DR.BETH LEIGH

# A happy and healthy marriage

# Contents



1.

2.

3.

4.

5.

6.

One

# Chapter 1

## WHAT MARRIAGE IS ALL ABOUT

Marriage also called marriage or wedlock, could be a socially and frequently lawfully recognized union between individuals called companions. It builds up rights and commitments between them, as well as between them and their children, and between them and their in-laws.[1] It is considered a social all inclusive, but the definition of marriage changes between societies and religions, and over time. Ordinarily, it is an institution in which interpersonal connections, more often than not sexual, are recognized or authorized. In a few societies, marriage is suggested or considered to be obligatory some time recently seeking after any sexual movement. A marriage ceremony is called a wedding.

Individuals may wed for a few reasons, counting legitimate, social, libidinal, enthusiastic, budgetary, otherworldly, and devout purposes. Whom they wed may be impacted by sexual orientation, socially decided rules of inbreeding, prescriptive marriage rules, parental choice, and person want. In a few ranges of the world,

1

organized marriage, child marriage, polygamy, and constrained marriage are practiced. In other ranges, such hones are banned to protect women's rights or children's rights (both female and male) or as a result of worldwide law.[2] Marriage has verifiably limited the rights of ladies, who are in some cases considered the property of the spouse. Around the world, fundamentally in created vote based systems, there has been a common slant towards guaranteeing rise to rights for ladies inside marriage (counting canceling coverture, liberalizing separate laws, and transforming regenerative and sexual rights) and legitimately recognizing the relational unions of interfaith, interracial, and same-sex couples. Contentions proceed with respect to the legitimate status of hitched ladies, tolerance towards savagery inside marriage, traditions such as share and bride cost, constrained marriage, eligible age, and criminalization of premarital and extramarital sex. Female age at marriage has demonstrated to be a solid pointer for female independence and is persistently utilized by financial history research.[3] Marriage can be recognized by a state, an organization, a devout specialist, a tribal bunch, a nearby community, or peers. It is regularly seen as a contract. A devout marriage is performed by a devout institution to recognize and make the rights and commitments inherent to marriage in that religion. Devout marriage is known differently as hallowed marriage in Catholicism, nikah in Islam, nissuin in Judaism, and different other names in other confidence conventions, each with their possess limitations as to what constitutes, and who can enter into, a substantial devout marriage.

# Two

# Chapter 2

## IMPORTANCE OF MARRIAGE

10 Reasons why you should get married

For those who are married or those planning to get married, you might find yourself relating to the following positive reasons for getting married.

### 1. Marriage will give you the legal rights of a spouse

We all know how important it is to be the legal spouse not because you want your children to bring the legitimacy of their birthright, but it plays a vital role in your assets and all kinds of marital rights, including retirement funds and alike.

Still wondering why it is important to get married, read on!

## *2. Marriage is the beginning of your new life together*

Marriage is not just a legal union. It is both a physical, spiritual, and emotional alliance as you and your spouse will now decide together and will no longer think selfishly but rather for the benefit of your family.

It gives you and your partner a legitimate chance to commit to your relationship.

## *3. Marriage teaches you the importance of commitment*

Though many marriages indeed lead to divorce because of affairs, many couples have successfully defeated this temptation.

Wouldn't you treasure what you have with your spouse if you're married? Wouldn't you think twice about ruining your marriage just because of temptations?

## *4.Marriage will strengthen your union as a family*

Let's face it – it is easier to abandon your partner and your child when you're not bound by marriage.

Statistics show an alarming rate of an absentee parents, which will then cause significant mental and behavioral effects on a child.

When you are married and have kids, even if you're facing problems, there are more than enough reasons for you to rethink your priorities and life.

*So, why get married- It's still one of the building blocks of a healthy family. And, you ought to strengthen your relationships for a happy and fulfilling life.*

## 5. It is the ultimate act of love for your partner

If you truly love someone, won't you imagine your future with them? Won't you dream of building a family with your partner and binding it with marriage? Would there be any other reason you won't marry the person you love?

It's one of the strongest glue that any couple can have aside from commitment, respect, and love.

## 6. Marriage is not the last step towards a happy ending

Marriage doesn't work for some and ultimately leads to divorce. But, people still know how sacred marriage is and know the importance of getting married.

A marriage, of course, isn't the last step towards that happy ending but rather the first step in making your own love story, which will require lots of patience, understanding, commitment, love, and respect.

## 7.Marriage provides a deeper level of connection and intimacy

When people get married, they create a relationship that gives them safety and security and a sense of belonging together. Marriage lets you create a spiritual, emotional, mental, and physical connection with your partner that grows stronger with time.

You can be honest and vulnerable with your partner and still feel safe and content.

## 8.Marriage creates a synergy

The oneness that comes with marriage allows a couple to become better even with their differences. A married couple with a united vision can be unstoppable.

Marriage allows you to dream together and work towards it side by side. It gives you support for a lifetime, and with this assurance comes the confidence to achieve extraordinary things.

## 9.Lifelong support system

Imagine how often you felt alone when you were single and struggling through hurtful things in life. Marriage is the best support system that one can have.

You will always have a person to share everything in your life with. Your significant will always be there to share all the parts such as happiness, mood swings, work troubles, life hardships, etc. They will not only listen but will also provide you with a different perspective.

## 10. It provides your relationship a place in society

No matter how many years you have beendating, most people will consider your relationship casual unless you are married. You might have been living with the person you are dating and be never taken seriously.

*However, marriage gives a socially acceptable name to your relationship. It helps you celebrate your love for one another. It creates your presence as a strong couple in society and provides the needed respect from society.*

Three

# Chapter 3

# Six Purposes for Marriage?

$G$od designed marriage to fulfill six important and vital functions. When we understand them, we will be better able to honor marriage.

## 1. Companionship

True companionship grows out of a oneness of spirit. This occurs in marriage when both the husband and wife can say, "My spouse is my best friend." "Can two walk together, except they be agreed?" (Amos 3:3).

## 2. Enjoyment

The principle behind enjoyment is self-control. "Marriage is honorable [precious] in all, and the bed [should be kept] undefiled: but whoremongers and adulterers God will judge" (Hebrews 13:4).

## 3. Completeness

God designed Eve to complete that which was lacking in Adam's life. "And Adam said, … She shall be called Woman, because she was taken out of Man" (Genesis 2:23).

## 4. Fruitfulness

God's first command in Scripture is this: "… Be fruitful [bear fruit], and multiply [increase], and replenish [fill] the earth …" (Genesis 1:28).

The very nature and character of God is to multiply life, whereas the nature and character of Satan is to multiply death.

## 5. Protection

A husband is to protect his wife by laying down his life for her. (See Ephesians 5:25.) A wife is to protect the interests of her home. (See Titus 2:4–5.) Parents are to protect their children to raise up a Godly seed.

## 6. Typify Christ and the Church

Marriage is to be a human object lesson of the divine relationship between Christ and believers. (See Ephesians 5:31–33.).

Four

# Chapter 4

# Healthy Marriage

## What is a "Healthy Marriage

Healthy marriage is the type of marriage that has these qualities stated below.

*Commitment*. Spouses in healthy marriages are committed to each other. They are dedicated to the partnership and maintain a long-term perspective so that short-term problems don't threaten the marriage.

*Satisfaction*. In healthy marriages, both individuals are satisfied. About 90% of married people say they are satisfied with their marriage. This is not because their marriages are void of problems, but rather because both spouses are committed to persevering through both good and difficult situations.

*Good Communication*. Using clear communication to solve problems is one of the strongest indicators of healthy relationships.

***Effective Conflict Resolution***. Individuals who have established healthy marriages are able to resolve conflict effectively. Spouses who effectively overcome stress and conflict are able to avoid criticism, contempt, and defensiveness from their marriages.

***Lack of Violence and Abuse***. In healthy marriages, spouses never use aggression or violence to gain control over each other. This includes, but is not limited to, verbal, physical, emotional, and sexual abuse. They also never abuse or maltreat their children.

***Fidelity or Faithfulness***. In healthy marriages, spouses are sexually and emotionally faithful to each other. On the other hand, infidelity is one of the most common causes of divorce.

***Intimacy and Emotional Support***. Spouses who are intimate, emotionally supportive, trusting, and caring have healthy marriages.

***Friendship and Spending Time Together***. In healthy marriages, spouses act like best friends and spend quality time together. Couples often have different hobbies, but a key indicator of a healthy marriage is that couples enjoy each other's company and have a respect for one another.

***Commitment to Children***. Spouses who are both committed to their children tend to enjoy more enriching marriages.

***Duration and Legal Status***. Spouses in healthy marriages believe in the permanence of their relationship. They are more likely to stay together when faced with difficult life circumstances.

# Five

# Chapter 5

# U NHEALTHY MARRIAGE

*signs of an unhealthy marriage*

All these signs are what we see in an unhappy and unhealthy marriage.

1. **Your partner is too critical or insulting toward you.** Although healthy criticism is always productive, if your partner finds faults with everything you do or say, it may be the time to reflect on their motive. Furthermore, advice with good intentions is made in privacy.

2. **You no longer share or enjoy intimacy.** Intimacy is a crucial part of marriage. It breeds emotional and physical connection and a sense of belonging. If you and your partner are not getting intimate as much as you used to, it is not a healthy sign.

3. **You are preoccupied with the idea of separation.** If divorce or separation is on your mind most of the time, you may need to ponder why is this happening. An unhealthy relationship may make you fantasize about divorce regardless of how difficult separation can make your life.

4. **You feel too controlled by your partner.** If it is your partner who decides what you should wear, how you must behave, or what you should eat, it is a sign that they are trying to control you. A healthy marriage involves giving the other person enough freedom to decide for themselves.

5. **You no longer seem to have meaningful conversations.** Every time you decide to talk, it turns into a heated argument or an ugly war of words. Communication is the backbone of any relationship and if this bridge is broken, the individuals are doomed to fall apart from the relationship.

6. **You feel too lonely.** Even if your partner is around, you feel like you are alone. An unhealthy marriage may make you crave care and concern that you do not get from your partner anymore.

7. **You disregard each other's priorities.** Be it food, rest, or a vacation, you or your partner do not care for what the other person wants. You may be working a night shift, but your partner does not care if you get enough rest the following day.

8. **You do not trust them anymore.** Trust and loyalty are what make people stay. In an unhealthy marriage, you are not each other's confidante. Rather, you seem to hide things from each other.

9. **You find it difficult to respect them.** Respect ensures that your relationship lasts and you value each other. If you do not respect your partner or they do not respect you, it may indicate an unhealthy and weak relationship.

10. **You do not feel commitment in the relationship.** A successful marriage means falling in love with the same person over and again. If you do not feel the commitment toward your partner, it indicates an unhealthy marriage.

11. **You cringe at their company.** You feel that you are better alone because everything they do or say is so intolerable to you. Cringing or disliking each other to this extent must not be overlooked.

12. **You feel neglected.** Your partner may neglect you by not being attentive to what you say. They may care about what others in the family feel but not pay any heed to your emotions or wishes.

13. **The relationship is hampering your personal or professional growth.** A healthy marriage is one where you help each other become better. If your marriage is holding you back or preventing you from becoming a better version of yourself, it sure is unhealthy.

14. **You feel that you get no space in the relationship.** You may be closely bound by your relationship, but you both are still unique individuals. If you feel too suffocated by your partner's interference, it means that your marriage is not healthy.

15. **You seem to "unhate" them.** It is said that indifference and not "hate" is the opposite of "love." You or your partner do

not seem to be bothered by each other. You do not care what
they say or do. Even the arguments seem unnecessary and
any response is futile. These signs may indicate a dying
relationship.

Six

# Chapter 6

# Top Tips for a Healthy and Happy Marriage

It takes work to have a healthy marriage but it is possible. Just like good nutrition and regular exercise can help you have a healthy body, there are things you can do to have a healthy marriage. Here are 10 tips to strengthen your marriage:

- **1. Spend Time with Each Other**
- Married partners need time together in order to grow strong. Plan regularly scheduled date nights and weekend activities. If a getaway is not immediately possible, then make it a goal that you will work toward. By spending time with your partner, you will better understand your differences and how to negotiate the problems they may cause. Forget the "quality vs. quantity time" discussion—healthy marriages need both.
- **2. Learn to Negotiate Conflict**
- Conflict is a normal part of any relationship. There is a point, however, when it can increase in intensity and become

emotionally and sometimes physically unsafe. Working out problems in a relationship starts with understanding what your issues are and how to discuss them. There are many resources available to help you learn how to deal with conflict. Using these resources can go a long way in preserving how safe you and your partner feel.

- ### 3. Show Respect for Each Other at All Times
- When a couple fails to respect each other they often slip into negative habits. Research shows that nothing can damage a relationship quicker than criticisms and put-downs. Treating your partner as you would like to be treated will strengthen your bond. Paying your partner a compliment is a quick and easy way to show them respect. When you are tempted to complain to someone about one of your partner's flaws, ask yourself how you would feel if they did that to you?
- ### 4. Learn About Yourself First
- Make it a point to work on self discovery. Many partners enter into relationships without knowing enough about themselves. As a result they can also have difficulty learning about their partners. Learning about yourself will better equip you to grow as an individual and a partner. Regardless how long you've been together, there are always more things you can learn about him or her. What are his dreams for the future? What is her worst fear? Imagine the bond you will share over a lifetime together if you commit to discovering new things about one another!
- ### 5. Explore Intimacy

- Marital intimacy can open your relationship to a whole new level of enjoyment and closeness. It is important, however, to remember that intimacy does not always mean sexually.An often forgotten aspect of intimacy is the emotional type. An example of emotional intimacy is creating a safe space for your partner to share his/her emotions without fear of judgment or ridicule. Learn the difference between emotional and physical intimacy and when each one is most appropriate. Offering your partner one type when they really need the other can create problems in your relationship.
- **6. Explore Common Interests**
- Couples thrive when they share similar interests. That doesn't necessarily mean each partner will enjoy every activity but it opens up the opportunity for greater sharing and compromise. Doing things separately is not bad but common interests are important to healthy marriages. A common interest may be cooking or eating new foods together, going for walks or playing cards. The goal is to have something outside your family that you both can enjoy.
- **7. Create a Spiritual Connection**
- Many couples grow closer when they share some form of spiritual connection. This can be done in many different ways. For example, it may be through an affiliation with a church, synagogue or mosque, through meditation or by simply spending time in nature or intimate conversation.
- **8. Improve Your Communication Skills**
- The ability to talk and listen to each other is one key to a healthy marriage. You should never assume your partner

knows what you are thinking or feeling. Tell your spouse what is going on—and as a spouse, know when to simply listen. Learning to really hear your partner is a skill that may require practice. There are many resources available like books, marital education workshops and online courses. All of these options can help couples learn how to communicate more effectively.

- ### 9. Forgive Each Other

- If he or she hasn't already, your partner is going to do something that hurts, frustrates or upsets you. Guess what, you are going to do the same thing! Sometimes it might even be on purpose after an argument or misunderstanding. Forgiveness is a tricky but important virtue in a marriage especially since no one is perfect. Try to allow your partner some room to make a few mistakes because you will also make some of your own. When you make a mistake, act quickly to apologize and fix problems. Doing so will help to encourage forgiveness and strengthen your marriage.

. ### 10. Look forthe Best in Each Other

When you met your partner, you fell in love with some of his/ her wonderful qualities. Over time however, your view of those qualities may have changed. For example, he may have been really good at saving money when you met. Now you just think he's cheap! Give each other the benefit of the doubt and create a list of all the things you love about your partner. It will help you to fall in love all                              over                              again!

# Seven

# Chapter 7

Here are 15 verses to hold on to.


1. Ecclesiastes 9:9 says, "Enjoy life with your wife, whom you love, all the days of this meaningless life that God has given you under the sun—all your meaningless days. For this is your lot in life and in your toilsome labor under the sun."

2. Ephesians 4:2-3 says, "Be completely humble and gentle; Be patient, bearing with one another in love. Make every effort to keep the unity of the spirit through the bond of peace."

3. 1 Peter 4:8 says, "Above all, love each other deeply, because love covers a multitude of sins."

4. Hebrews 13:4 says, "Let marriage be held in honor among all, and let the marriage bed be kept pure, for God will judge the adulterer and all the sexually immoral."

5. Ephesians 4:32 says, "Be ye kind one to another, tenderhearted, forgiving one another, even as God for Christ's sake hath forgiven you."

6. Psalms 127:1 says, "Except the Lord build the house, they labour in vain that build it."

7. Ecclesiastes 9:9 says, "Live joyfully with the wife whom thou lovest."

8. James 5:16 says, "Therefore confess your sins to each other and pray for each other so that you may be healed. The prayer of a righteous person is powerful and effective."

9. Mark 10:9 says, "Therefore what God has joined together, let no one separate."

10. Ephesians 4:26 says, "Let not the sun go down upon your wrath." "

11. Colossians 3:19 says, "Husbands, love your wives, and be not bitter against them."

12. 1 Corinthians 13:4-7 says, "Love is forbearing and kind. Love knows no jealousy. Love does not brag is not conceited. She is not unmannerly, nor selfish, nor irritable, nor mindful of wrongs. She does not rejoice in injustice, but joyfully sides with the truth. She can overlook faults. She is full of trust, full of hope, full of endurance."

13. Proverbs 21:19 says, "It is better to dwell in the wilderness, than with a contentious and an angry woman."

14. Romans 12:10 says, "Be kindly affectioned one to another … in honour preferring one another."

15. 1 Peter 4:8 says,"Most important of all, continue to show deep love for each other, for love covers a multitude of sins."